KINGDOM, PHYLUM

KINGDOM, PHYLUM

Adam Dickinson

Brick Books

Library and Archives Canada Cataloguing in Publication

Dickinson, Adam, 1974-
        Kingdom, Phylum / Adam Dickinson.

Poems.

ISBN-13: 978-1-894078-54-2
ISBN-10: 1-894078-54-3

        I. Title.

PS8557.I3235K56 2006   C811'.6   C2006-902307-7

We acknowledge the Canada Council for the Arts, the Government of
Canada through the Book Publishing Industry Development Program
(BPIDP), and the Ontario Arts Council for their support of our
publishing program.

 Canada Council   Conseil des Arts
for the Arts   du Canada   Canada
ONTARIO ARTS COUNCIL
CONSEIL DES ARTS DE L'ONTARIO

Cover image by Victor Brauner. Loup-table (1939-1947). 54 x 57 x 28.5
cm. Centre Pompidou, Paris. © Estate of Victor Brauner / SODRAC
(2006). Photograph courtesy of Art Resource, New York City.

Author photograph by Judy Townson.

The book is set in Minion and Bodoni.

Design and layout by Alan Siu.

Brick Books
431 Boler Road, Box 20081
London, Ontario N6K 4G6
www.brickbooks.ca

For my family,
my first order

Contents

Good

Some people dismiss taxonomies and their revisions as mere exercises in abstract ordering—a kind of glorified stamp collecting....No view could be more false and more inappropriately arrogant. Taxonomies are reflections of human thought; they express our most fundamental concepts about the objects of our universe. Each taxonomy is a theory about the creatures that it classifies.

— Stephen Jay Gould

This, however, is the sublime melancholy of our lot that every You must become an It in our world....Genuine contemplation never lasts long; the natural being that only now revealed itself to me in the mystery of reciprocity has again become describable, analyzable, classifiable...

— Martin Buber

Density

All things desire
to be as close as possible.
So planets form as spheres.
So the lost walk in circles.
Smoke leaves a fire clinging to the faces of those who stand over it, curling
in the anxious arcs of changing state.
The table is set in the capital. The tsar sits to a meal of round beets, globes of
bread, and the circular livers of ducks. Let us eat he says, but cannot. His
stomach turns.
So hell has circles, Dante tells us.
So the damned may still cling, so they may eat.
A stone dropped in a still pool makes concentric rings. Gravity is not inert,
it is not without need, or caprice, or folly. At all costs, things lie down. They
wish to touch. The water marks this wish with waves. Diminution.
So the sound of footsteps comes from everywhere.
So a pulse has the acoustics of dream when it is dark, when you are making
for home.
Wolves encircle deer. Deer contain wolves, they are chemistries of
undergrowth, winter die-back, and winter in the hips and legs, and winter
breaking into the cedars making the boughs taste resinous, making the deer
taste like paved roads, like coins, and everything is crowded together. How
quickly what is becomes dance, becomes feast.
So the sun makes a wheel in the sky.
So clocks take the form of wide eyes, open mouths.
History repeats itself. Great loops in the goings and comings, in the heart
attacks and treaties, the agricultures that start again in the dim mornings
where hedgerows suddenly have the look of long graves.
The hands on the clock go around.
The hands return easily to the mouth without thinking. This is how we
contain ourselves.
Sadness is a cold front in the lungs, the air contracts, snow clouds line the
soft pink coasts.
Ecstasy is a thermal vent, breath escapes through your palms, newly
vertebrate islands stand out of the ocean. Teeth glint through spreading
fingers.

So it is written from dust to dust.

So there lies between summer's open-windowed wit and winter's mineral pensiveness the autism of spring and fall, the equinox, where, for a moment, with expressionless face, things could go either way.

Cars spin out in the rain, in the snow. Do doughnuts.

Accidents happen on the drive back home.

So when the rain has passed there are always three rainbows. The first two are easy enough to see, spooning each other like sediment, a record of the changing light, the wavelengths that passed on, collected in the air like primeval forests, bodies.

The third rainbow is always behind you, circling the sun. There the archive is kept; where the visible has its own halo.

So the stations of the cross go around. Repeat.

So water will cross over itself. Oxbows. The Mississippi, The Saskatchewan, Mackenzie River Delta.

So the phases of the moon are lessons in composition.

What she meant to him falling asleep in the car as he drove back from the city. The deer that stood in the dark at the side of the road. How he stopped to watch them gather in the field, and she surprised him with touch, and the moon that lit her face, a daylight of rooftops and speechlessness.

So strength returns with rest; every task a departure.

What is it within us that we learned so well in the caves, what reflex climbs out of our hunger, wraps around that place in the brain where language assembles, where it rises out of the rocks, a passion, a staff?

What we learned from the boulder.

So prayer makes us thicker, brings this world to the next.

So food makes us thicker, brings this world to the next day, intestines are a ministry, wells dug in the tablelands.

Food augers through the coils of dry need.

So a sphere is the largest volume with the least surface area.

The smallest commitment to the outside.

Hedging has form:

I love you, but as a planet—like the farthest ones of spun gas—in case you get too close, in case you open the careful tectonics of my bare arms.

So electrons go around the outside.
Two trailer park girls go 'round the outside.
So I love you. I love you; a stutter
is desire balled in the mouth, pure roundness, language of the infinite O.
So even light curves in on itself, catches in the throat.
So it drags its waves great distances, taking thirty years to leave the star
Arcturus and arrive in a pair of binoculars in a clearing of barren rock and
spruce on a night in August where you are with your family, who have lived
away from you for years, who have grown older, have gathered their lives
about them in woollen blankets, in windrows of touch, and there above you
all, like a photo album, the house being built, a song from the 70s, is all the
time that has gone before.
Arcturus gives light from the year you were born.
So a wave is a circle proposed and withdrawn, proposed and withdrawn.
The ocean touches the coast with stutter.
The sun reaches a period of indecision each night, drinks, smokes—whatever
it is the circular do to continue.
Starlight touches your family; the Great Lakes curve around you like sleeping,
slow-breathing dogs.
Starlight is the outside of a tree, the oldest part that cracks, that can't contain
water, the image that slowly arrives, milk that comes up from the ground in a
faint chain of globes.
So the brain was once a stem
before we crowded it with wonder.
A single stem before joblessness, child poverty indexes, downtown
redevelopment projects, arterial service lanes, lobes of *laissez-faire*.
Tell me, what do you do?
The hippocampus says rise, eat, have sex, stand in a high place, lie down
under cover and sleep.
It says I do. There is no outside, no delegated tasks, no facility for the genius
salesman.
So the brain has spheres, so the mind wanders from room to room
trying to feel at home, rearranging the furniture, tilting the pictures to
various angles of down.

If you're crossing the equator in a boat
and you flush the toilet, which way does the water circle? How much of
descent has to do with attention? We go down without looking; our boots
take in water thoughtlessly.
The moon on the river is small scoops.
Fish curve in their muscular tattoos returning at night to the bugle of eddies.
So we eat.
The outside comes in.
So chromosomes coil,
making each of us a fist, cupped hands, holding some smaller, older stone
that has been passed down like spring seeding, a family blanket, patched and
re-stitched; a telephone game where the message becomes confused,
So I have always loved you. I said I loved you.
So.

I

Angle

It is interesting that in many mythologies,
Time is a god: but never Space.

— Jan Zwicky

Syncline, Anticline

Syncline, anticline:
headed up, or headed down?
How do you know if you've reached
the midpoint of your life,
whether from here the stairways creak,
or a new agriculture comes closer?
This shortness of breath,
might be folding tents,
the earliest camps of air closing down;
these sore hands, the first exaggerated fingerprints
of soaking too long in the bath.

Obtuse, acute:
gawp, glance, or hard stare?
Certainty is density's oldest illusion;
the lake in winter, its thin ice cocksure,
water light-headed with crystal;
the irresistible exoskeleton—
folded arms, cooled fat in the roasting pan,
burnt wood throbbing to gas in the coals
of a finally vertebrate life.

Incidence, reflection:
How does sympathy move among us?
Thunderstorms rust in the valley,
they are nervous systems for working things out,
for giving off light that is only equation.
Every decision is a wishbone,
a false dialectic of uneven halves.
It's not how hard you pull, but how long
the bones have been left to dry.

Contributions to Geometry: the Snake

Not simply the garden, the machinations
of splitting such right-angled rules.
Its body is line, but not railroad, or light,
not telephone wire or bridge.
It moves as wilful smoke, leaving the ash of a life
angular as wood, curling up, each curve
a science of forgiveness.
It thinks: forget those crosses and boxes
in the crystals of freezing, in the hardening of death.
To move through the world is to bend, is to give.

Before straightened rivers, there are oxbows.
Before the grid roads of quitting your job, moving to the city,
and trying to find her, there are
the intestinal ribbons of your brain,
the twisted chromatin of sex, the lives
whose scrawled arcs unwind before you
like the coiled spring of a clock.

Philosophy Is Going Uphill

Feet planted, one after the other,
climbing is syllogism,
the world being built beneath each step,
truth tables locked in the knees.
Someone climbs with you and both of you are breathless,
as though each chest were a grasp,
as though holding hands meant
thinking the same thing.

Downhill is memory—slack rope,
spilled drink.
Most of the body is water;
knees can't be the only answer.
They are red herrings, swimming,
fallacies of the undistributed middle:
all stars are fires, but not all fires are stars,
all weight is gravity, but the knee
descends creek beds without proof.

Coming down, you remember your life.
All the log cabins of thinking
lean dangerously,
suddenly much farther from town.
Downhill remembers mornings burnt with dark,
the river falling over itself like terrible news,
abandoning the higher ground,
the loose-footed stones.

Contributions to Geometry: the Gulf Stream

Hot : Cold

People in fires
crowd exits.

Lost hunters at night
climb inside the stomachs of deer.

Form is really
just accommodation.
The four dimensions
are four climates,
each with their own pressures,
and furniture.

Conveyor belt, heat pump, ribbon.

The sine wave of the seasons
has not always been so neat.
With every ice age the current slows, negotiations fail.
Tropic doesn't speak to pole.

Long before Columbus, strange woods and fruits arrived on the
    shores of Europe.
Hurricanes stayed alive until Ireland.
Postmaster Benjamin Franklin observed that the sea off Nantucket
did not sparkle at night.

Hot water and cold
are the accidents of organism.

Ice is not modern.
Our clothes become part of us.
Climate is a haircut or a shoe.

When the stream moves over the undersea mountains off New
    England,
the bottom is sheared off and giant gyres spin out to the east.
Beginnings resemble each other.
There is an exit at the front and the back.

Leaving for Toronto

Like biblical scholars, leaves
spend the summer translating light.
Does this mean fall is faithless?
Or is it the luminous seal into parchment,
the pages stiffened and folded?
What clutters the ground
            and sticks to our shoes are the very words
we use for going: you leave,
we leave without speaking,
or at least without words we can follow.

Now, that moment when nothing is written,
between dictations that are strewn and sodden,
wet spades blunt in the street,
and the first hard frost that announces—
            with the smoke you see in your breath—
that even heat translates poorly.
The snow comes down without scribes,
a faith of salt and glass.

Pairing

Already I have let wet balconies replace you,
astral tadpoles in the concrete,
anything.

Anything is the gerund leaking from reference,
that hard symbol-maker's pride, the cordillera
of stopping to stare.

How easily the uplands of certainty are forgotten,
giving way to the difficult glaciology
that grinds in what cools.

You make piles around me—salmon climb upstream,
rusted railings, their headstrong bodies are
bloodied fists.

What is left is the reversed punch line
of taking two stairs at a time,
the light heart that sinks at the top, the conclusions

that dissolve like city pavement
into premises for ghetto, for back lanes,
these amphibious stars of cracked cement.

Pattern: Four Sides

Art begins not with the flesh but with the house.
— Gilles Deleuze and Félix Guattari

A.

Artefacts grip the museum.
Alphabets.
Artichokes belong to the legumes.
Aristotle came from Stagirus, or Stagira, or Stageirus.
After the Indian Wars the Buffalo Soldiers continued to distinguish themselves,
achieving medals of honour in the taking of San Juan Hill.
Agamemnon was murdered in the bath by his wife.
Above Agawa Bay are pictographs carved into cliffs;
animals figured in afterlives.
Anishinabe, Assisi, astronaut.

B.

Babylon hangs its gardens.
Bark slumps from the birch.

Before any of this, before luxury and fortification, before Mesopotamia, Hammurabi,
banishment, before Cyrus, and the seven Popes, there was a single river that dreamt
bluntly out of the mountains, hanging silt in its current, smashed stones.
Better to suffer in this life for riches in the next.
Buffalo soldier in the heart of America.
Blue is the shortest of the wavelengths.
Blacks, browns, whites, and reds show up in Palaeolithic cave paintings,
but no blue. Barely any influence, the sky.

C.

Christ took three days to recompose.
Carbon molecules look like triangles.
Carpentaria the gulf. Carpathian the mountain.
Calculations by Irish Archbishop James Ussher in 1650 claim to identify the date of
creation based on the ages of biblical prophets: October 26, 4004 BC.
Cygnus is the swan in the northern hemisphere between Hercules and Pegasus.
Clearing his throat, the Benedictine monk waits silently for bees
coming in from the canola fields.

Caraganas split their pods.

Cyan is a mix of green and blue.

D.

Determinism.

Donnybrook.

Desire is a banana peeled and eaten in the snow.

Dictum of Harvard President Larry Summers: "In the history of the world no one has yet decided to wash a rented car."

Dad washes them.

Darwin tells us that absolute ignorance can take the place of absolute design.

Delta, the fourth letter in the Greek alphabet, is earth and alluvium deposited at the mouth of a river in the shape of a triangle.

Discipline is dry spells.

Contributions to Geometry: Cold Hands

Prior to oblong and isosceles,
and the butterfly knife of Pythagoras,
someone fumbled with wood for a fire,
holy orders came square from fingers,
angles broke and healed in the knuckles.

Cold hands are the opposite of splinters,
the numb occupancy of belief, the outside
that sticks you from within, blood
hardening, having seemingly abandoned you,
having turned to lumber clotting the lakes.

But blood opens its star-shape
in the bristles of your joints,
in the solar reminder that, outstretched,
buffooned with cold,
every touch has five sharp points.

Cryo

Cold begins in the ears by breaking sticks,
its first small fires carefully set.

Listening cools the body, cracks glass,
broken storefronts downtown,
the mouthfuls of empty street,
the echoes that throb in those
who wake suddenly, branches
high-pitched at the window.

Listening is crystallography,
fingers over piano keys, waxwings:
pointillists in the mountain ash.

The cold comes in as dendrites,
as words that split like the beds of rivers
in lowlands where the sea hears only salt.

Our lips are parched in the wind.

We sleep in different buildings.

These conversations are better held with noise.

The Meteorology

for bpNichol

there is an H in Alberta
over the foothills
high pressure
sun
in Hinton, Hobbema, Yellowhead

L's come from the Pacific
born in Aleutian longitude
                                 coldfront libido
leguminous

a bright idea is a cumulous, a bunch of lightbulbs
crowded together
over Medicine Hat

but an inkling is a circus, a cirrus, a wispy S
composed,
like all high clouds,
of horse hair and halos

a mackerel sky
a tuna fish sandwich
a man could do worse than let the outside in

A Body of Too Many Spines

We are, for the most part, on our hands and knees,
like the rain creeping into a house;
thin needles of the hydro-cycle,
the part that begs to come indoors
and implicate each of us.
We come to error with the nudity of benches.
All our summers have the same beginnings,
bright ideas slice themselves open like fruit.
We are horseshoes making blacksmiths.
We are too many fires.
New wood and the old wood;
the past isn't so much remembered as turned into fuel.
What is the opposite of forgetting?
Justice? Swallowing the wrong way?
It can't be remembering.
We are always remembering,
there are very few subjects that tolerate our memory.
We are the aftermath;
treelines driven to drink in the heat.
Resemblance falls to the ground pointing everywhere.
We are not the hardwoods we like to think,
but the more primitive conifer,
its bundle of needles,
a body of too many spines, too many ways to stand.

Contributions to Geometry: Lichen

Because there is no such thing as a single beginning.
Before crowberry and fireweed, among ruined boulders
that the ice let go, this slow committee.
Even now in the city, on the bark of big-boned ash,
small coastlines of lichen
are the end of the Wisconsin,
fresh melt water pooling, fingerprints plotting
new hands.
Here, in the bullish confidence of bark,
evidence that even trees
wear the beginnings of later trees.

Think of yourself as an agreement:
arms and legs in step,
each cell holding up the walls of another.
Your language is a minority government
where backbenchers rise suddenly,
threaten to cross the floor,
and what comes from your mouth
is a difficult vote.
There are two sides to every story.
North that must think south. Somewhere
in your gut other lives
remind you
with fever, stiff joints, with dream.

Join or Connect in the Carpenter's Sense

Most of us   are born indoors,
but are buried   outdoors.
This is the consolation   of nature poetry,
lyric hands on the shovel,   wet pitch on the pine.

For the earth, air, angel, and mortal   there is a private sun.
Each stands in the daylight   with dedicated trilobites hunched in the bone.

The earth prays in lava domes,   in dolomite on foggy coasts;
the air in cumulonimbus,   lenticular Chinook clouds;
the angel in his breast,   in her song, a round stone smoothed in the throat.

For the mortal there are Sundays and the pious floods of spring rivers,   there are
hands hung out the sides of car windows   opening and closing like gills
in the pickerel streams, like viruses   in tired animal circulation.

Daylight is as heedless as a countertop,   an armload of clothes;
the mortal cuts wood and splits   it into planks, into the latent heat of bridges, rafters.

But in the evening when the private sun   has turned to its own personal life
and the dark is a man on his knees,   the invertebrate work of prayer
on his lips,   the mortal lies down among purposes for sleep,
the constellations   of board and nail, food and cupboard.

At night we go outside and there the angels   polish igneous in the domes under cirrus.

We dig   to come back indoors.

II

Hour

What then is time? I know what it is if no one asks me what it is;
but if I want to explain it to someone who has asked me,
I find that I do not know.

— St. Augustine

Precambrian

That hand-worn banister in the brain,
that Lake Superior stone long past molten, yet
still the muscle-memory of drip, of
thinking before skin,
before tropical tail feathers,
the bone on bone of getting here.
Try putting the key in the door at minus twenty,
fingers pitched with cold.

When finally, after years of wanting her,
she comes into your life,
you can only respond with the molasses of dream,
with the waterlogs of bulrush.
It is sediment hereafter
and the anticline of your attention
that can manage only toast in the mornings
and eating directly from jars.

Things grow old in two ways: they harden
and they soften. Density is that moment
when touch wears clothes in the lake,
and your lover's arms jellyfish around you.
It is what grows in the body—a body itself
unable to protest
the stiffened igneous, or the muddy shore
that grip might become.

Cambrian

Even when there is no life, there is
going through the motions.
Mud stumbles out of the hills
oxygen-starved,
small stones lay themselves down like seasonal fat;
you get ready for winter without thinking.
I love you on the lips like stacked wood.
Six washed apples glint on the table
where light makes small windows,
far from the tree, far from the glassworks
of sun and rain, the lives before fossils.

Of course, even when there is no death,
there are the preparations.
Not all of your breath leaves when you breathe,
a little remains in each gasp, holds back.
So finally—when the mouth is dry
and the hydraulics of looking are drained—
microbes brown in the blood;
meat and potatoes turn, apples turn.
In your body a small pocket of air,
a bundle of sticks, some matches.
When you go, you must go, be gone.

Palaeozoic

Shells began as waste
worn on the outside of the body,
slow corals that grew as the uselessness inside
made its way to use, to irony.

But it's hard to say how skeletons came about,
or why they first grew on the outside.
Early intention, perhaps, certainty
migrating to the surface of the skin,
the decision to move to the city, a bricklayer.

Why? So you could push back?
Bones were the early memories of rock,
the impossible nostalgia,
mineral homesickness, heavy heart.

There is a small bump on your collarbone.
I know now it was the start of a new decision,
the slow radial wish of ribs
away from me.

Carboniferous

We lean heavily on the same routine, the flesh,
fumbling hands,
like a few words in a foreign tongue.
Cheque, please. Where is the train station?
We are the early carboniferous,
the first great decadence: trees reclining
at the edge of a shallow sea.
"As for living, our servants will do that for us."
We drink, lie down, turn to oil.
The train is across town.
Da kommst du von hier nicht hin.

Belief is the imagination as coal, a foreleg
just entering a clearing—
ignition of leaps, the woods spark with departure,
smoulder with the certainty of what has been.
Tonight there is work to be done;
downtown, the coal smokestacks bulge
as though they were the thinking ends of trains,
the dark clouds of speechless deadfall.
Don't believe in cool steel ashes,
fine new leaves.
At night we lie down in the shallows
again and again until the imprints of our bodies
fill with what has overflowed us.
Wet hands.
Ten hearts.
Quelle heure est-il?

Upper Pleistocene

In the beginning, heaven was divided from earth,
night from day, sea from dry land.
I watch dark birds fly south
like collapsed roofs, like wide-open mouths.
I watch them leave the city of split streets,
the poplar branches leaning away from each other.
Maybe in the beginning He saw that it was good,
but it wasn't.
You are born, limbs grow away from you,
leave home.
All the king's horses, all the king's men.

Look, creation says, your body has split:
arms, legs, fingers. Bones of the inner ear
may have evolved from the jaws of snakes
that crept up to make listening
out of teeth, and out of hunting,
speech.

This house is haunted, the pipes
shake water up from the ground.
Ripped shingles must be dark birds,
a rail spur, blind alleys of evolution:
go back to the ocean, the birds say,
go back to that place where you chose to have joints,
chose choosing. It's not flight you want,
but to come home,
lie down, be together.

The Egg as Immigrant

Eggshells were the earliest suitcases,
carefully packed bags.

Homesick had its shape:
one end less eager than the other,
broadening downward,
an album of wet plans
opened and pored over.

How long does it take to say
that you have always been here?

Mammals thrust their eggs
deep within warm inland flesh,
as if to renounce the struggle
of their own immigration,
thin and humble luggage that once salted them
with scales.

The egg moves in humans now
like creeks filled and buried in the centres of cities,
their passages jerked to the network of sewers.

It travels once a month
in the fertile interval lands;
the blood that emerges, also pushed underground,
unspoken.

Gravity, the egg-shapes of rain
uncommitted to the sky.

We arrive holding on
to where we've been:
           into any gushing wound,
you can pump seawater
and a body will continue to live.

Toward what new land will something yet
compose its shell

and climb out of our moisture,
the shape of its doubt
unevenly glistening at the edges of our eyes?

A Chemical History

The eel is dedicated to direction,
a body hastily drawn, an emphatic map
where details are assumed.
Effortlessly it avoids any hands,
any legs, any evidence of beginning.

Here is what we know:
eels are born in the ocean at certain times of the moon
on the tops of undersea mountains.
Following the schematics for salmon,
they migrate into fresh water,
up rivers plugged with dams, into the begged questions
of highland watersheds, the mud-filled seasonal pools.

After years, after enough time for people to believe
new sandbars have emerged at night in the silted streams,
they come back down to the ocean, their bodies loose socks
filled entirely with sex, with current, no need for muscle or bone.

Not even the ancients, their hands thick with beginnings,
could ever find any eggs.
Eels came from bits of skin, they thought,
horsehairs accidentally dropped in water,
vegetables rotted right through.
Aristotle said they came from mud,
from poorly drained ground.

To catch an eel, you must put aside everything
you know about fishing.
Even the water.
On a cool, rainy night an eel lives on land
long enough to slip between stream beds and lakes,
between the black pools of the ditch.

For anyone who lives near a river,
an eel has been in your basement;
their tubular bodies are a rolled message
from the beginning:

No one remembers being born.

When you walk at length in the rain,
it is easy not to notice
the mud that flicks at the backs of your legs.

Time My Lips, My Blue Hands

Late at night, you can't sleep.
The quiet carpentry of shadows.
What you worry about arrives on a train,
crowds the platform like soldiers.
There is snow and coal dust in the air.
The particulate of night, the sand of darkness,
on uniforms, in hair, the grit between your teeth.

The problem of history is the problem of reference.
You were there. No, you were *there*.
The first snowflakes that come down in the fall
are ashes, burned plans.
You had been this certain.
But late at night with the train coming in,
with the commotion on the platform,
you feel the cold in your lips, in your hands.
Time is the alternating current of boots,
the rails, the bodies before you
that make no effort
to hide their tracks.

For the Structures, I Miss You

In approaching the other I am always late for the meeting.
— Emmanuel Levinas

Fast.
Fasting.
Hunger crawls through the body
checking its watch.
Inwardly magpies call
reaching the bells of your chest, the fresh strokes
of their rooting in empty cans,
dull jangling fence posts and stems.
How long has it been?
There is no definition in the gut;
what you want is a quantity of pendulum,
a mouthful of swing,
to be held in someone else's clock.
Whatever breathes, breathes you,
exchanging inert landscapes,
the *long ago*
that had, without notice, drifted
into uprooted pavement, illegible hands,
into the present that climbs on itself like frost,
a window churning up in the stillness
of freezing.

Haunting is a lapse of fresh experiences.
There are noble notes, noble gases
in the sublime,
and you remember the clear air
that surrounded what you loved
with height and depth, with formality.
A past where clothes worn up mountains
were removed in the meadows by swimming hands.
Your synthesis is vague now,
imagination flattened, humbled,

no longer dominating the universe
with its suspension bridges,
cataracts, and cliff dives.
A sentimental mind tries to pass
for someone else's ghost.
The magpies peal swiftly within you.
Hungry, perishable,
fast.

Mnemonic

Kingdom, Phylum, Class, Order, Family, Genus, Species.

Karma peels cautiously off falsely genuine statues.

Keats' principally claimed: odes forever grow sodden.

Kayaks paddle, canoes orient, fish gather scholastically.

Keep praying conscience outlives favour (given sycophancy).

Keys pry chords open, flattening generic signatures.

Knowing philosophy can't ornament faith's galvanic simplicity.

Kill plants carefully; our future goodwill's shapeless.

III

Good

(a) belonging to the Emperor, (b) embalmed, (c) tame, (d) sucking pigs, (e) sirens, (f) fabulous, (g) stray dogs, (h) included in the present classification, (i) frenzied, (j) innumerable, (k) drawn with a very fine camelhair brush, (l) et cetera, (m) having just broken the water pitcher, (n) that from a long way off look like flies.

— Michel Foucault

The Good

The good itself could be a mushroom,
may wear a crown after all,
require a certain humidity: logs,
tree stumps, bathroom tiles,
those cumulus brains
in the late afternoon
over hot prairie towns.

No one can explain the sickles
of dead grass in the yard
when mushrooms leave.
A revolution without hammers.
No one can say what goes wrong
when, half-hearted, attention divided,
we can't bring ourselves to finish
our holy designs.

The greatest moral works
are mushrooms.
They reveal themselves as this.
Take the Bible, take
the Geneva Convention.
Look at the curves of dead ground.
Take the Communist Manifesto;
it needs very little light.

For some time, we expected
the end of the world
to be a mushroom.
A vengeful good, a good
of fire, clouded thought.
But every spring they come out of the ground

like universal suffrage,
a writ of *habeas corpus*,
speech before writing.
They say, dirt. They say, get up.

The Unreflective, the Inland Fish

Attention squats in your head,
in the old amphibious part of the brain,
a fish climbing ladders to the silt beds,
the plans for forgetting your keys
so you have to return to her house.
The city outskirts, with their oil tanks
and broken trucks, their food-coloured car lots
have the curious fertility of flood plains.
This is where thinking leaves us, a reflection
messed by the wind on the water into the stars of a punched eye,
into the drunk calcium of the strip mall.
This is the end of explanation, the amazement
that in the high plains, beyond the ocean's strict piano,
there are trout in the hardwater streams.
How do you explain the spokes and pulleys that winch
the knot in your gut? The face that swims
through the curtains at night, its question composed
entirely of mouths?
Like the horizon, like the flesh,
what divides us from the unknowable
is a wet mouth, the middle distance of explanation.
The flags by the car lots are stiff. The wind
has dragged its fish bones into town.

Father Demetrius's Bees

All day over the canola,
small prayers for the sun.
If love could quit its veins, its chemical language,
the airy transmogrification of trembling hands,
the clots that build dark hills in the chest,
it would be these small sparks, these lanterns
that explain plants to each other,
that return home at night,
and write the first desires of things
in moonlit sugar.

Because we cannot simply stand in the sun,
because there is no single honeysuckle,
no hummingbird tuning the valves of the heart,
they work in the name of abundance.
To live is to stick to things, honey in the hands,
the simplest wish crowded with wings.

It is said that when the beekeeper retires,
he becomes allergic to the venom of bees.
What love asks so much?
All day over the canola,
the fresh wax of introductions,
the first deposits of fat
in the catacombs of the heart.

Kingdom, Phylum, Class

The trees are starting to change here as I'm sure they are in Toronto. Yesterday on my walk I found a white ash that was so golden people had to squint while walking under. Closer to school I couldn't ignore the deep purple on that bush just outside your old office. I often think of you. Recently, I read of a species of bower bird so convinced of the perfection of its own colour that everything it builds is similarly shaded. It weaves together blue wrappers and blue straws and its own blue feathers. But this nest is only for show—displayed on the ground to attract a mate. After they come together, the female builds a sensible nest, camouflaged, high in the trees.

It's raining here today and the yellow ash leaves lie in the street waiting for someone to put a peach or a pineapple together. This is, I guess, the job of the peach bird. Maybe commitment is love that has discovered taxidermy, or taxonomy, I could never keep them straight. Maybe it's both—thinking that is stuffed and sorted. What do they use anyway? To stuff I mean. How could you replace the insides? I'm sorry. I'm sorry. The rain has soaked the red shirt you gave me. Where are the red-breasted birds?

There were once eight deadly sins. Four corners, four sides. Mistakes were square buildings on angular croplands. The good was a grid. Intersections of four-way stops. What was wrong could be piled in columns, or extended away from the body in diminishing rows. For this reason early towns were low to the ground. Where buildings went up, they stooped to avoid undue attention to the necessary back alleys, the long curved shadows. Gluttony, greed, lust, wrath, envy, pride, sadness, and sloth. Bad decisions were combinations, sturdy staircases that rose over the land like genomes. Over time, interest in the shape of problems was replaced with a greater concern for their number. Just as Newton had to distinguish between indigo and violet so the rainbow could be made of seven, Saint Gregory in the Middle Ages merged sadness with sloth to make the sins add up. Sloth now carried the work of two—the only sin for which no pardon could be granted. The slothful are not lazy, but hopeless. If we stand in rows before God, then sloth marks figure eights in dust on boots, creases in pant legs. It is sin without architecture. Not even holes in the ground. Where once there were corners, walls, ladders and towers, now bad decisions have no outside—no cornfields, no drive into town. The seven sins twist around sloth, lean and fall inward. They are not blocks but a Möbius strip, a coiled rope hanging nothing. What is the shape of a mistake? Do not abandon your head to the support of your hand.

Practice

Nothing flies occasionally. If you do it, you must do it constantly;
so the reason for migration is not magnetic, not desire
for an endless summer, but necessity, the belt and pulley of practice.
A lifetime of pianos: all cows eating grass.

We are obsessed with falling down. It's in every story we tell. We stand on two legs
to tempt fate: the gods must eventually give us flight or weigh upon us
with bricks and bibles, amendments and presidents.

Graves are six feet deep because for so long we believed that in death
we still had room to stand underground and rehearse
for wings. We were shorter then. Now we hunch,
and look down. One clay foot trembling in front of the other.

The Dumb Anonymity

The ears are charged with balance.

To listen carefully is to drink with both hands.

To miss you is the weight of apples, fallen
among the bent grasses at night, an organ
whose machinery is pulp.

We stand upright

because we do not ignore the stars,

their pin weather,
the gravity of having eaten fruit.

The first high Sirius at dusk is enough
to tie your shoelaces together.

The Good

Take two hands.
Clasp them.
Prayer, or cold weather?

Originally, thought was fat
travelling through the body
in small spoons, in sensible corridors;
it was warm and clear,
needed to be liquid to fall
in its pure logic
through the systole and diastole,
the parentheses of what one has
and wants.

By the time it reached the hands
the pipes had cooled, thickened into confusion,
the earliest nonsense,
the first figurative language.
Fingers numb with fat
and grasp.

Some argued the good was soap,
fat foaming out of hands under water,
touch so slippery and quick
that it had to be right.

Others saw a grease fire,
a pan tipped by unsteady hands,
an accident in the kitchen,
over the hearth, where suddenly
blisters rose like cupped palms
to a mouth.

It turns out soap will burn.

Cut it into thin strips, pile it
into the shape of a house,
strike a single match.

It clarifies as it melts, leaving a thin flame,
drawing darkness around it and a part of the eye
that can see stars
only by looking away.

Islands Hesitate at the Mouth of a Bay

One way to think
is dry land.
A body, an outcrop,
breast into the wind,
birds are the only exchange.
But even here, corporality is pneumatics,
clockwork is a pine
bent at the waist by wind,
the shore comes down like the bottom of a voice.
                        Shallow lagoons
salted with flies, can bear no weight;
words sink wet feet
between posts and analyses, driftwood
and mosquito bites, between
signatures and scratch.

The atom is illustrious.
A city of so much land it is a planet.
Mechanical philosophies drive cars
through the streets, engines revved
and rigorous.
Out in the bay, islands wear specular sunlight,
meteors burn in insolvency.
The body is a radiant species.
Think flood.
Think Leonid, Perseid.
Planets that have broken
fall to us,
repeat their appearance
as the humble inconsequence of worlds.
Dry land aches with cloud.
The islands are shapeless
and still.

The Humours

1.

Blood, sanguine,
he loves you.
He'll take the detours of your name,
the homonyms, haemoglobins,
mortal dangers that herringbone
in the rudiments of subjects,
and write glowing letters in which the earth is mostly air,
the body mostly liver,
and cursives obey the first rule of heraldry: the sky must always intervene,
no metal upon metal,
nor colour upon colour.
His voice is thick with the confidence
and prophesy
of salt.
Blood has regular tides,
reference is a comfortable bed.

2.

Phlegm, phlegmatic,
doesn't hear you; the brain is cool,
a proper balance between dullness
and fever.
How can I make you love me?
They say a woman is easily filled with phlegm,
that its gloves loosen the biles within her
and an English winter sets in,
rain falling in quick, straight blades.
Too often, returning home at night
through the dampness,
eyes sharpened on the blunt range of his sloth,
she wipes her nose on her sleeve.
But this isn't right, it isn't her.
What else do you do with a phlegmatic man
but break into his chemistries?
The humour isn't in us, but around us;
take your clothes off carefully.

3.

Yellow bile, choler,
bilious, no one knows what will happen.
I can never see you again.
That's it.
The other humours blacken,
turn the lights out, and
step into the street with their ripped shirts.
It's the hottest day of the year,
a drought stretches over town making rubble of remembrance;
garrisons in the simplest thoughts
crowd the fruitless shade
to look for trespass and brimstone.
The gall bladder has quit,
I cannot write you;
coronas glisten my hands with new work.
Save yourself,
be neither flare nor throat.

4.

Black bile, the melancholic,
assembles his life,
puts together hummingbirds, the sad steam of their wings,
the mania of trying not to move.
He writes letters where sentences of looping capitals
run like rivers through old cities
full of bandages and cranes.
High minds hang in the square,
the river courses below in affliction,
its whole body moving night and day
in allegory, in algebra.
Bile feeds the spleen and thickens the blood.
But when the melancholic's body is opened,
instead of a heart,
we find split-necked shovels
in the dry grass,
a pile of twigs over the entrance to a hole.
It's too late,
he is gone.
And has been
for some time.

Vespers

The first difficulty is air,
its empty rooms, its cupped hands.

Breathlessness is a trap
sprung in the throat,

wearing clouds
on the inside of the voice.

Prayer makes high cheekbones of the air.

By wanting, by wishing,
the breath assumes a flesh of ears

in the diminished chords of dusk.

But like all earthly faiths, there is only the heat
of having already spoken.

Eclipse

Anecdote is the lowest form of evidence
that medicine will consider.

But stories grow out of the sick;
narratives hatched from the generative eggs
of endings.

There is a psychological condition
where people cannot be kept
from looking at the sun.

Night is suffocation
by the planet's
weight and width.

We are more like plants than we care to admit.
Rain is exchanged in our hair
as it is in the pine and broadleaf crowns.
We hunch down; the business of water
takes us into our bodies,
old messages stem in the spine.

A plant, a person,
is the small story of a place,
an anecdote of acid or lime.
Larger conversations of boreal and palm
contain such dialects of shadow,
rock face blocking the sun.

Solar complex. Solar plexus.
Freudian slip.
What is wrong with us
gives itself away in broad daylight,

in the very words that grow
from hands to mouths.

As in Latin,
disaster: the unfavourable aspect of a star,
a great or sudden misfortune.

Great Chain of Being

Linnaeus connected the world through teeth,
beaks, and bills.
This was the point where one thing entered another:
minerals the appetite, voice
the open air.
Ornament entered function.
And so it was that the vernacular languages of Europe were insufficient.
Only Latin or Greek;
other tongues were dark and crowded.

Chokeberry seeds must first pass through the intestines of black bears.
In abundant seasons, a sow comes upon the patch on the open edge of
a riverbank. While chewing, something provokes her to turn suddenly
upstream and brace herself against a rock. This small amount of anxiety
stimulates enough acid in the stomach to break down the hard shell of
the berry seeds.

The mouth is the symbol for a corner.
Phoenicians built the alphabet out of joints,
sounds whose shapes in the throat and lips
were translated into sticks
piled or bent on the page.
Small fires grew.
People stood at windows to watch,
arms outstretched.
For the Greeks this was epsilon;
for the Romans the letter E.

Cough then glottal stop,
heartbeat then iamb,
marshland then coal
then greenhouse.
All bells are held at the top,

just as all plants are tied to the sun, just
as language, despite its vacuums and cinder blocks
hangs above heads,
rings in the ears.

Sometimes in Canadian forests small pale plants stick up in clusters
from the ground with flowers that hang from their tops like bells. These
are pine-saps, ghost plants, or corpse flowers. No Kingdom will accept
them (neither plant nor fungus) because they are vascular organisms
that do not need the sun: plants with no chlorophyll, mushrooms with
rudimentary leaves. Aboriginals pick *eyebright* for the eyes; European
settlers, *convulsion weed* for the nerves.

Linnaeus read the atlas wrong
and gave plants in the high Andes
names derived from the arid New Mexican plains.
Nature doesn't jump.
Kingdoms are carefully spaced ladders
against the sides of burning buildings.
One rung at a time,
women and children are the first to descend.
If the final goal of creation is us,
then why for the index of berries in a small pamphlet
did Linnaeus write: "too sour"; "black and unpleasant"?

Unlike most birds, he said, swallows do not migrate during the winter
months to warmer southern latitudes. Instead they gather in the late fall
at the margin of cold lakes and estuaries. Here they plunge themselves
over the edge of the ice and pile on the bottom like hibernating frogs. If
you come upon a lake full of swallows and break the ice in the parts
that are darkest, the birds will appear in their masses, cold, asleep, and
half-dead. If you fish one out and warm it with your hands, it flies away
too soon. Every hole beneath it mistaken for an opening.

Homo sapiens was a draft.
So was *Homo diurnus.*
Both were crossed out and reinserted.
Well before Darwin, Linnaeus put us in with apes;
the only difference he could see
was in the canine teeth.

Whatever is, is right.
This is not an order but a riddle,
not a single thought, but many.

Notes

The first quote on page [9] by Stephen Jay Gould is from his foreword to *Five Kingdoms: An Illustrated Guide to the Phyla of Life on Earth* by Lynn Margulis and Karlene V. Schwartz (New York: W.H. Freeman, 1988).

The second quote on page [9] is from Martin Buber's *I and Thou* (Trans. Walter Kaufmann. New York: Charles Scribner's Sons, 1970).

The italicized line from "Density" on page 13 is from Eminem's song "Without Me."

The quote from Jan Zwicky on page [15] is from *Wisdom & Metaphor* (Kentville, NS: Gaspereau Press, 2003).

The epigraph to "Pattern: Four Sides" by Gilles Deleuze and Félix Guattari on page 24 is from *What Is Philosophy?* (Trans. Hugh Tomlinson and Graham Burchell. New York: Columbia University Press, 1994).

The italicized line in section "B" from "Pattern: Four Sides" is from the song "Buffalo Soldier" by Bob Marley.

St. Augustine's quote on page [35] is from *The Confessions of St. Augustine* (Trans. Rex Warner. New York: The New American Library of World Literature, Inc., Mentor-Omega Books, 1963).

The epigraph to "For the Structures, I Miss You" by Emmanuel Levinas on page 47 is from *Otherwise than Being: Or Beyond Essence* (Trans. Alphonso Lingis. Pittsburgh: Duquesne University Press, 1998).

The quote by Michel Foucault on page [51] is from *The Order of Things: An archeology of the human sciences* (London and New York: Routledge, 2002).

The italicized line from "Great Chain of Being" on page 73 is from Alaxander Pope's *An Essay on Man* [1733] in *Alexander Pope: Selected Poetry and Prose* (Ed. William K. Wimsatt Jr. New York: Holt, Rinehart and Winston, 1961).

"Great Chain of Being" is for Erin Knight.

Acknowledgments

Some of these poems have appeared in earlier versions in the following publications: *Breathing Fire 2: Canada's New Poets, Canadian Literature, CV2, The Fiddlehead, Listening with the Ear of the Heart: Writers at St. Peter's, The Malahat Review, Post-Prairie: An Anthology of New Poetry, Prairie Fire,* and *Sentinel Poetry* (UK). Some of these poems were also broadcast on CBC Radio One as part of *Alberta Anthology.* I extend my gratitude to all of the editors involved.

I wish to thank the Canada Council for the Arts, the Alberta Foundation for the Arts, and Dr. Catriona Mortimer-Sandilands, Canada Research Chair in Sustainability and Culture at York University for supporting the research and writing of this book. Special thanks to the Banff Centre for the Arts.

Thanks to my editor Gary Draper and to all of the fine people at Brick Books. Extra special thanks to Maureen Scott Harris for her patience, skill, and extreme generosity.

For help along the way with these poems, I thank: Adrienne Barrett, Barry Dempster, Don McKay, Steve McOrmond, Jan Olesen, David Seymour, Karen Solie, Charmaine Tierney, Matthew Tierney, Andy Weaver, and Gabrielle Zezulka-Mailloux. I owe an incredible debt of gratitude to Erin Knight for so much intelligence, generosity, and love.

Biography

Adam Dickinson grew up in Bracebridge, Ontario, and has recently lived in Edmonton and Toronto. He is now a professor of poetry and poetics at Brock University. His first book, *Cartography and Walking*, was short-listed for an Alberta Book Award. He lives in St. Catharines, Ontario.